Every Little Seed

By Cynthia Schumerth and Illustrated by Elisa Paganelli

PUBLISHED *by* SLEEPING BEAR PRESS™

Grandpa told Mom, and Mom told me:

The secret of a plant

lives in every little seed.

Spring sends a warm and
welcome breeze
that melts the winter snow.

It's time to plant our garden.
Can't wait to watch it grow!

Mom tills the earth as Grandpa rakes.
I pull out stubborn weeds.

The ground is soft and ready now,
a home for all our seeds.

I study every different seed,
each filled with so much knowing.
Everything they'll ever need
to keep them strong and growing.

And I think about what Grandpa told Mom, and Mom told me:

The secret of a plant lives in every little seed.

One by one and row by row,
each precious seed is sown.
Sun and rain will help them thrive.
We'll tend them 'til they're grown.

Garden Trowel

Garden Pruner

Shovel

Bulb Planter

Hand Fork

Claw Cultivator

Weeder

I gather up my garden tools,
now scattered all about,
and wonder when those tiny seeds
will send out roots and sprout.

Those clever seeds are busy,
beneath the ground unseen.

Already roots are burrowing,
and sprouts are turning green.

Soon plants stretch up and buds poke out,
young tender leaves unfurl.
Fragrant flowers start to bloom,
their sweet scents drift and swirl.

Cornflowers
and daisies

Petunias

Impatiens

Coneflower

Cleome

Hollyhock

And I believe what Grandpa told Mom, and Mom told me:
The secret of a plant lives in every little seed.

Our garden bursts with signs of life—
so many hungry guests!
Spiders spin their silky webs,
protecting plants from pests.

Bees gather pollen, buzz and hum,
sip nectar warm and sweet,
while flitting, floating butterflies
taste flowers with their feet!

Proud our garden's grown so well,
we sit back to enjoy it.

But then we spy invasive bugs—
they'll damage and destroy it!

They munch and crunch their garden lunch,
turn green leaves into lace.
The more we look, the more we find—
those bugs are everyplace!

APHIDS

We grab three cans and fill them up
with sticky, soapy water.
Then pick 'n' plop those hungry pests . . .
just one last bug—I caught her!

SOAPY WATER

JAPANESE BEETLE

BROWN MARMORATED STINK BUG

JUMPING EARTHWORM

When days grow short and nights grow cold,
our garden starts to thin.
As summer dances out the door,
fall knocks and marches in.

Leaves droop and curl, bright colors fade,
as dried-up petals fall.
But left behind are all those seeds,
dark specks that know it all.

We search through all the withered plants
and harvest every seed.
When spring returns, we'll plant again.
We'll rake and till and weed.

Sun's light will shine, soft rains will fall,
each seed knows what to do.
Our plants will grow and bloom once more—
pink, yellow, red, and blue.

And I won't forget what Grandpa told Mom, and Mom told me:

The secret of a plant lives in every little seed.

Let's Dig a Little Deeper into Seeds!

Some seeds are so tiny you can't even see them! Some are so large you need both hands to hold them. It may be hard to believe, but every seed—no matter how large or small—contains everything it needs to one day grow into a plant.

Most seeds have three things in common: a baby plant (THE EMBRYO), food for the baby plant (ENDOSPERM), and a covering (THE SEED COAT). The seed coat protects the embryo and endosperm until the seed is ready to grow.

Safe inside the seed coat, the baby plant waits until the seed gets just enough water and warmth to begin the growing process. It feeds on the endosperm until it is strong enough to push out roots and sprout. Seeds can lie dormant (sleeping) for many years as they wait for just the right conditions to grow. As long as the seed coat isn't damaged, most seeds can be stored for at least one year from the time they are harvested (collected) to the time they are planted. Many seeds can last two to five years, and some much longer. The oldest seed known to produce a plant was found in Russia. It is believed to have been buried by an Ice Age squirrel more than 32,000 years ago!

Seed Coat

Embryo

Endosperm

ORCHID PLANT

DOUBLE COCONUT SEED

THE BIGGEST KNOWN SEED IS A DOUBLE COCONUT SEED. (ITS SCIENTIFIC NAME IS **LODOICEA MALDIVICA**.) IT CAN MEASURE 16 TO 20 INCHES LONG AND WEIGH UP TO 40 POUNDS.

THE SMALLEST KNOWN SEED COMES FROM AN EPIPHYTIC ORCHID PLANT THAT GROWS IN THE TROPICAL RAIN FOREST. (ITS SCIENTIFIC NAME IS **ORCHIDACEAE**.) THIS ORCHID SEED IS SO TINY THAT WE CANNOT SEE IT WITHOUT USING A MICROSCOPE.

WHAT IS AN INVASIVE?

When insects, animals, plants, shrubs, or trees are introduced into a habitat that is not their native home, they are called invasive. They don't belong in this new habitat, and they have no natural predators (enemies) to keep their population under control. This allows them to take over their new habitat, destroying the native species that live there. We can help control invasive species by pulling out invasive plants before they spread, catching insects before they multiply, and capturing animals that don't belong. Always ask a grown-up to help with any of these actions so you can be sure to stay safe. Some insects can bite or sting. Some plants can poke you or cause a rash, and some are poisonous. And it's always best to leave animal catching to grown-ups. Stopping invasive species is not an easy task. But if we all do whatever we can to protect our native species from invasives, we will help them to survive and thrive.

SOME EXAMPLES OF INVASIVE SPECIES ARE:

JAPANESE BEETLES: INSECTS LIKE THE ONES IN THIS STORY; THEY DESTROY THE LEAVES OF PLANTS, SHRUBS, AND TREES

ROUND GOBY: A LITTLE FISH THAT EATS THE EGGS AND YOUNG OF NATIVE FISH

BUCKTHORN: A SHRUB OR SMALL TREE THAT SPREADS RAPIDLY, CROWDING OUT NATIVE TREES, SHRUBS, AND PLANTS

FERAL PIGS: WILD PIGS THAT EAT SEEDS AND DESTROY CROPS, DIG UP THE LAND, AND SPREAD DISEASE AND PARASITES TO NATIVE AND DOMESTICATED ANIMALS (LIKE COWS AND HORSES, AND EVEN OUR PETS)

THERE'S MORE TO SEEDS THAN GARDENING!

YOU CAN BE A DETECTIVE

Find a dandelion that has turned to fluff. Pick off some of the wispy white sections of the plant. Can you see the dandelion seeds? How do you think these seeds get from one section of your yard to another? What do you think you could do to stop dandelions from spreading?

YOU CAN BE A CHEF

After you carve this year's jack-o'-lantern, save the seeds. Wash and dry them. Then spread them out on a cookie sheet greased with olive oil. Swish them around, making sure both sides of the seeds are lightly coated with oil. With the help of a grown-up, sprinkle the seeds with salt, garlic salt, chili powder, or cinnamon sugar. Bake them in the oven at 400 degrees for 5 to 20 minutes (depending on the size of your seeds). Keep a close eye on them so they don't burn. When they start to turn light brown, they're done. Let them cool before you eat them! You can peel the shell off and just eat the inside, or you can eat the whole seed.

YOU CAN BE A NATURALIST
(a person who cares about nature)

YOU'LL NEED THESE ITEMS:
STRING, PINECONES, PEANUT BUTTER,
WILD BIRDSEED, AN ICE POP STICK OR SPATULA

Carefully tie one end of the string around the pinecone. Using your ice pop stick or spatula, cover the pinecone with peanut butter. Roll your peanut butter–covered pinecone in birdseed until completely covered. Hang your feeder outside to feed the birds.

For Judi, John, Mike, and Tim—
some of the best seeds ever planted
Love, Cindy

To all the plants that have survived my care.
I love you and I promise I'll keep trying to be a better plant-mom.
I would truly be lost without nature.

—Elisa

SLEEPING BEAR PRESS™

2395 South Huron Parkway, Suite 200, Ann Arbor, MI 48104
www.sleepingbearpress.com © Sleeping Bear Press

Printed and bound in the United States.

10 9 8 7 6 5 4 3 2

Library of Congress Cataloging-in-Publication Data
Names: Schumerth, Cynthia, author. | Paganelli, Elisa, 1985- illustrator.
Title: Every little seed / written by Cynthia Schumerth ; illustrated by Elisa Paganelli.
Description: Ann Arbor, MI : Sleeping Bear Press, [2023] | Audience: Ages 4-8. | Summary: "Told through rhyming text, three generations of a gardening family work together to bring a backyard garden to full bloom, from planting to caretaking to harvesting"-- Provided by publisher. | Identifiers: LCCN 2022036781 | ISBN 9781534112698 (hardcover) | Subjects: LCSH: Gardening--Juvenile fiction. | Seeds--Juvenile fiction. | Families--Juvenile fiction. | Stories in rhyme. | CYAC: Gardening--Fiction. | Seeds--Fiction. | Family life--Fiction. | Stories in rhyme. | LCGFT: Stories in rhyme. | Picture books.
Classification: LCC PZ8.3.S29743 Ev 2023 | DDC 813.6 [E]--dc23/eng/20220912 | LC record available at https://lccn.loc.gov/2022036781

Photo Credits:
Round Goby: Rostislav Stefanek | Shutterstock.com • **Japanese Beetle**: Mircea Costina | Shutterstock.com • **Wild Boar**: Volodymyr Burdiak | Shutterstock.com
Common Buckthorn: dcwcreations | Shutterstock.com • **Dendrobium Orchid**: Awana JF | Shutterstock.com • **Double Coconut Seed**: © Nigel Hoy | Dreamstime.com